THE REAL DEAL

Drugs

Rachel Lynette

Heinemann
LIBRARY

www.heinemann.co.uk/library
Visit our website to find out more information about Heinemann Library books.

To order:

☎ Phone 44 (0) 1865 888112

📄 Send a fax to 44 (0) 1865 314091

💻 Visit the Heinemann bookshop at www.heinemann.co.uk/library to browse our catalogue and order online.

First published in Great Britain by Heinemann Library, Halley Court, Jordan Hill, Oxford OX2 8EJ, part of Pearson Education.

Heinemann is a registered trademark of Pearson Education Ltd.

Editorial: Nancy Dickmann
Design: Richard Parker and Tinstar Design Ltd
Illustrations: Darren Lingard
Picture Research: Mica Brancic and Frances Topp
Production: Alison Parsons

Originated by Chroma Graphics
Printed and bound in China by Leo Paper Group

ISBN 978 0 431 90729 1 (hardback)
12 11 10 09 08

10 9 8 7 6 5 4 3 2 1

ISBN 978 0 431 90736 9 (paperback)
13 12 11 10 09

10 9 8 7 6 5 4 3 2 1

British Library Cataloguing in Publication Data
Lynette, Rachel.
  Drugs. - (The real deal)
  1. Drugs - Physiological effect - Juvenile literature
  I. Title
  613.8

A full catalogue record for this book is available from the British Library.

Acknowledgments
The publishers would like to thank the following for permission to reproduce photographs: Bubbles/John Powell p. **12**; Corbis/LWA-Dann Tardi p. **4**; Corbis Sygma/Alan Lewis p. **19**; Getty Images pp. **20** (Matt Cardy), **21** (Taxi/David Oliver), **24** (The Image Bank/ Ghislain & Marie David de Lossy), **27** (Taxi/Chris Sanders); Masterfile/Jeremy Maude p. **15**; Photofusion/ Melanie Friend p. **23**; PhotoLibrary.com/Bill Bachmann Photography p. **26**; Rex Features pp. **5** (Marja Airio), **11** (SAKKI), **13**; Science Photo Library pp. **6**, **7** (Adam Hart-Davis), **8** (Robert Brook), **9** (TEK Image), **10** (Gustoimages), **17** (Cordelia Molloy), **18** (Gustoimages), **25** (Deep Light Productions); SuperStock/Lisette Le Bon p. **22**.

Cover photograph of an arrow road sign reproduced with permission of iStockphoto/Nicholas Belton; cover photograph of a syringe reproduced with permission of Getty Images/PhotoDisc; cover photograph of pills and capsules reproduced with permission of Corbis.

The publishers would like to thank Kostadinka Grossmith for her assistance in the preparation of this book.

Every effort has been made to contact copyright holders of any material reproduced in this book. Any omissions will be rectified in subsequent printings if notice is given to the publishers.

Disclaimer
All the Internet addresses (URLs) given in this book were valid at the time of going to press. However, due to the dynamic nature of the Internet, some addresses may have changed, or sites may have changed or ceased to exist since publication. While the author and publishers regret any inconvenience this may cause readers, no responsibility for any such changes can be accepted by either the author or the publishers. It is recommended that adults supervise children on the Internet.

Contents

Some words are shown in bold, **like this**. You can find out what they mean by looking in the glossary.

What are drugs?

A drug is a substance that changes the way a person's mind or body works. Drugs can change the way a person feels, thinks, and behaves. Drugs can help a person who is sick, but they can also cause serious damage and even death if they are not used correctly. There are many kinds of drugs, and people take drugs for many different reasons.

Many people take drugs when they are sick or injured. People can purchase **over-the-counter drugs** such as cough syrup and aspirin at pharmacies and most supermarkets. When people have a more serious illness or injury, they may need to use a drug that is prescribed by a doctor. Over-the-counter and **prescription drugs** can help people with their medical conditions, but it is important to use these drugs as directed. When these drugs are used inappropriately, they can be harmful.

Prescription drugs should only be used under the care of a doctor.

People use many kinds of drugs recreationally.

Recreational drug use

Some people use drugs recreationally. Recreational drug use involves using prescribed or over-the-counter drugs in ways not directed or in using **illegal** drugs. People use drugs recreationally because they like the way the drugs make them feel. Recreational drug use is not only illegal, but it is also dangerous and often **addictive**. The only way to use drugs safely is to use them under the care of a doctor or other responsible adult.

Top Tips

It is important to use and store drugs safely. Here are some drug safety tips:

- Always take drugs as directed.
- Never take someone else's medicine.
- Tell an adult right away if you think the medicine is making you feel sick.
- Store all medicines in their original, labelled containers.
- Store medicines where children cannot get them and use child-resistant caps.
- Throw away outdated medicines.

Types of drugs

There are many different kinds of drugs. Most of the drugs that people use recreationally fall into one of the seven categories explored in this chapter. Illegal drugs are sometimes called street drugs.

Cannabis

Dried leaves and flowers from the hemp plant are used to make **cannabis.** People who use cannabis usually smoke it. Cannabis is sometimes called dope, pot, grass, weed, or marijuana. Cannabis gives the user a mild feeling of **euphoria,** and is addictive for some people. It can also be a **gateway drug.** This means that people who use cannabis are more likely to go on to use stronger drugs.

Case Study

Ethan started using cannabis when he was 13 years old. At first it was just on the weekends with friends, but soon he started smoking it every day. Smoking cannabis became the most important thing in Ethan's life. He felt sick, irritable, and depressed on days when he could not get any.

Cannabis comes from the hemp plant. Its leaves are easily recognizable.

Cannabis is a Class C drug. This is the lowest class of illegal drug, but it is still illegal to possess or sell it. Just possessing the drug could lead to a prison sentence of two years. **Supplying** the drug to other people could result in a prison sentence of up to 14 years.

Depressants

Depressants make the user feel relaxed. They make the body work more slowly and can make a person feel drowsy. Some are used to treat **anxiety** and sleep disorders. They are legal when prescribed by a doctor. Depressants include Valium, Xanax, and tranquillizers. They can be called downers, moggies, or tems. Depressants can be addictive. Alcohol is also a depressant.

NEWSFLASH

Xanax, a prescription drug, is often abused by teenagers in the United States. At a school in Philadelphia, several students were taken to the hospital after taking Xanax pills. The pills were brought to school by a 13-year-old who had taken them from a relative.

Many depressants, such as Valium, come in the form of pills.

Solvents

Solvents are substances which have fumes that can be inhaled. There are many different kinds of solvents. They include paint, nail polish remover, and model glue. When their fumes are inhaled they cause a feeling of euphoria. Using solvents in this way is called solvent abuse. On the street it is sometimes called sniffing or biffing.

Solvents are extremely dangerous when inhaled. They can cause permanent damage to the brain or to other parts of the body. They are extremely addictive. They can even cause immediate death. **Sudden sniffing death** can occur any time a person abuses solvents.

Common household products can cause serious harm and even death when their fumes are inhaled.

NEWSFLASH

Studies have shown that parents can decrease the chances that their children will use drugs just by talking about them. Unfortunately, many parents either do not know what solvents are or do not understand that they are dangerous. As a result, they may not talk to their children about them.

Hallucinogens

Drugs that cause **hallucinations** are known as **hallucinogens.**
They cause severe behavioural, mood, and personality changes.
Hallucinogens include LSD, PCP, and some kinds of mushrooms. They
may be called acid, angel dust, or shrooms. Most hallucinogens are
illegal. Hallucinogens are usually taken by mouth.

Although hallucinogens are not addictive, they can have very negative
side effects. A user may have a "bad trip." This means that his or her
experience might involve frightening hallucinations and intense feelings
of panic, anxiety, or depression. During a bad trip, a person might try to
hurt themselves or others.

People who have used LSD may also experience **flashbacks.** A
flashback is when someone experiences the same sensation they felt
when using the drug long after the effects of the drug have worn off.
Flashbacks can occur weeks, months, or even years after the last use of the drug. In addition, using hallucinogens can cause permanent brain damage.

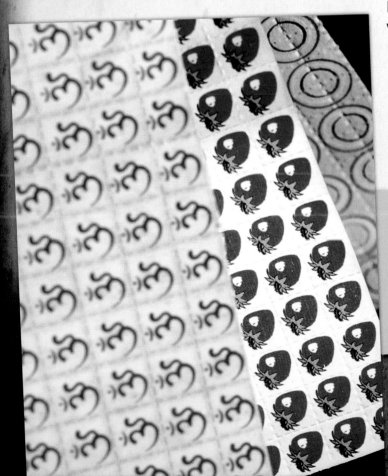

These colourful squares may look harmless, but each one contains a dose of LSD.

Stimulants

Stimulants make the body work faster. They increase alertness and energy, and can give the user a feeling of euphoria. Uppers, speed, crack, meth, and X are street names for stimulants. Some stimulants are prescription drugs that are used to treat medical conditions. For example, people with Attention Deficit Hyperactivity Disorder (ADHD) may have trouble focusing and concentrating. Stimulants can help them. Stimulants are also used to treat obesity. These drugs are legal when used as directed.

Crack, cocaine, methamphetamines, and MDMA (Ecstasy) are illegal stimulants. Stimulants are often used recreationally and are very dangerous. Stimulants can cause violent behaviour, **paranoia,** and anxiety. They can cause permanent harm to the body and the brain. In addition, stimulants are highly addictive.

NEWSFLASH

Children with ADHD are often prescribed the stimulant Ritalin to help them stay calm and focused. But some children sell their Ritalin pills for illegal use. Schools and parents need to make sure that prescription drugs are only taken by the children to whom they are prescribed.

Cocaine is usually snorted through the nose, while crack is most commonly heated and smoked.

People who use heroin usually inject it directly into their bloodstream.

Opiates

Opiates are drugs which come from the opium poppy. They include morphine, codeine, opium, and heroin. China white, gear, and smack are some of their street names. Doctors prescribe some opiates because they are very effective in relieving pain. Opiates can also give the user a feeling of euphoria. Opiates are extremely dangerous when used recreationally, and are highly addictive. Heroin is one of the most addictive drugs in existence.

Anabolic steroids

People take **anabolic steroids** to increase body mass and build muscle. Some steroids are legal for medical uses. However, some people take steroids illegally to enhance their athletic performance or appearance. Anabolic steroids can be called roids, gym candy, stackers, or pumpers.

Steroid use can be very dangerous, especially for young people. Steroids can permanently stunt growth. They can cause cancer, kidney damage, high blood pressure, high cholesterol, and severe acne. They may also cause extreme mood swings, aggression, and depression.

Why do people use drugs?

Most people use over-the-counter drugs for minor medical problems. They use drugs prescribed by their doctor for more serious medical conditions. Even though it is illegal, people of all ages use drugs recreationally. Most recreational drug users are teenagers and young adults.

Most people start using recreational drugs because they enjoy the "high" drugs give them. The drugs may create feelings of euphoria, energy, or relaxation. But people often do not realize that the drugs they are using are dangerous and addictive.

In 2004, a survey found that the most common reasons for first using an illegal drug were curiosity (65 percent) and **peer pressure** (44 percent). Many teenagers start using drugs because of peer pressure. They may think that using drugs will help them fit in and make friends. Teenagers who give in to peer pressure and use drugs are breaking the law. They are putting their health and maybe even their lives at risk.

Peer pressure is often a factor in recreational drug use among teenagers.

NEWSFLASH

Studies have found that some kinds of anti-drug adverts may actually increase drug use. This is because rather than making teenagers think about the risks of using drugs, the adverts make them curious. Adverts that work best focus on the positive aspects of not using drugs.

Singer Justin Timberlake has admitted to using recreational drugs.

Celebrity drug abuse

Teenagers are influenced by people they admire. When they hear about celebrities using drugs, they may want to use them too. Singer Justin Timberlake surprised and disappointed his fans when he admitted that he has used drugs. Dwain Chambers, an Olympic sprinter, received a two-year ban from athletics after testing positive for using steroids. In 2005 supermodel Kate Moss was filmed using cocaine. Her drug abuse cost her several modelling contracts. Some celebrities, such as actor River Phoenix, have died from drug **overdoses**.

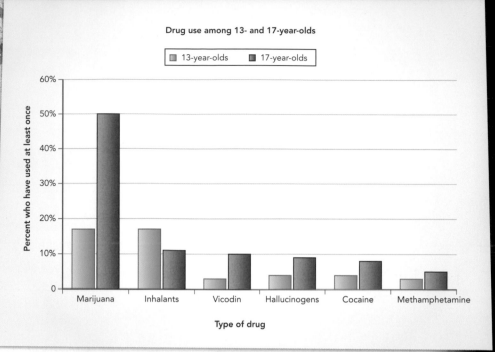

This chart shows the percentage of teenagers that have tried different types of drugs.

Popular drugs

Cannabis is the most frequently used illegal drug. It is also the first illegal drug that many young people try. About 11 percent of 11–15 year-olds in the United Kingdom have used cannabis in the last year.

Solvents are popular with younger children because they are inexpensive and easy to obtain. About 4 percent of 11-year-olds reported using solvents in the last year while only 1 percent had used cannabis. Although solvent sniffing itself is not against the law, it is a crime for someone to supply a solvent to anyone under 18 years old. It also accounts for between 70 and 100 deaths in children every year.

Recently, the number of teenagers abusing prescription and over-the-counter drugs has increased. Often, teenagers get these drugs from their own homes. Using prescription drugs inappropriately is dangerous and illegal.

NEWSFLASH

A recent study found that more teenagers today are abusing prescription and over-the-counter drugs than illegal drugs. One reason for this is that many teenagers mistakenly believe that prescription drugs are safer and less addictive than illegal drugs.

Case Study

Legal penalties for using or selling drugs can be harsh. Michael, an eighteen-year-old, was arrested for selling a small amount of cannabis to an undercover police officer. He now faces a fine and up to 14 years in prison.

Drugs and the law

Recreational drug use is illegal in the United Kingdom. Every year thousands of people are arrested for using, possessing, and selling illegal drugs. People who are caught with drugs may be subject to community service, fines, and jail time. People who sell drugs or who are caught with large amounts of drugs can face long sentences in prison, including life sentences.

Selling and using recreational drugs is against the law.

How do drugs affect people?

A drug's effect depends on many factors, including the kind of drug, how much was taken, the way it was taken, and the user's unique body chemistry. Drugs can be swallowed, smoked, inhaled, or injected. No matter how drugs are taken, they always end up in the bloodstream and are carried to every organ in the body, including the brain.

Short-term effects

Drugs work by changing the way the brain makes or uses chemicals. The chemical changes in the brain affect the way the person thinks and feels. Drugs also affect the way the body works. Some drugs speed up heart rate and increase alertness, while others slow it down and cause relaxation.

What do you think?

Some schools conduct random drug tests. Supporters say that the tests stop children using drugs and help identify those who need help. Others say that the tests can be inaccurate. This could give parents a false sense of security or wrongly accuse children of taking drugs. Do you think schools should give drug tests?

Drugs can be taken in different ways.

Drug	Street Names	How Taken
Cannabis	pot, grass, weed, dope, marijuana	smoked or eaten
Solvents	using is called "sniffing" or "biffing"	inhaled
Amphetamines	speed, uppers, billy whizz, whites	swallowed, inhaled, or injected
Methamphetamine	meth, crank, crystal, yaba, chalk	smoked, swallowed, or injected
Depressants	downers, moggies, tems	swallowed
Cocaine	coke, snow, dust, toot	inhaled
Crack	freebase, rock, gravel	smoked
LSD	acid, blotter, microdots	licked or swallowed
MDMA	ecstasy, XTC, E, love doves	swallowed
Heroin	smack, horse, junk, skag, gear	injected, smoked, or inhaled
Steroids	juice, roids, gym candy, stackers, pumpers	swallowed or injected

Smoking cannabis can make it difficult to think clearly.

People who are high on cannabis will feel a mild feeling of euphoria and may have trouble thinking clearly. They may not be able to finish a sentence because they forget what they are talking about. **Coordination** can also be impaired and heart rate increases.

Solvents cause a feeling of euphoria that has been compared to being drunk. Effects may include slurred speech, loss of **inhibition**, and impaired coordination. Solvent abusers can experience serious negative effects the first time they use the drug, or any time after. These include headache, vomiting, unconsciousness, heart and brain damage, and sudden death.

Drugs such as crack, cocaine, methamphetamines, LSD, ecstasy, and heroin are very powerful. Their effects are very intense. A person using these drugs might become suddenly aggressive or very depressed. They may try to hurt themselves or others.

Long-term health effects

Using drugs recreationally even just one time is dangerous, but long-term drug use is even more dangerous. In addition, long-term use of most drugs results in addiction.

People who regularly smoke cannabis are likely to become depressed. They may lose interest in normal activities and may have trouble relating to other people. Heavy cannabis use has been shown to affect concentration and memory, making learning difficult. Some of these problems may not go away, even if the person stops using cannabis.

The long-term effects of solvent abuse can include severe personality changes. A user could become angry, violent, or depressed. He or she may also feel anxious and have difficulty remembering things. Frequent abuse of solvents may cause weight loss, muscle weakness, and organ damage.

Using drugs can cause depression.

NEWSFLASH

A 2006 study found that heavy users of cannabis performed poorly on memory tests even when not using the drug. When asked to recall words from a list, frequent cannabis users could only remember an average of 7 words out of 15. People who did not use cannabis performed much better, averaging 12 words out of 15.

Case Study

Megan started abusing solvents when she was 12. She stopped doing her schoolwork and started lashing out at other people. She even hit her mum. Megan got help and has been clean for two years, but she still has serious memory problems. Sometimes she forgets what she was talking about just a few seconds earlier.

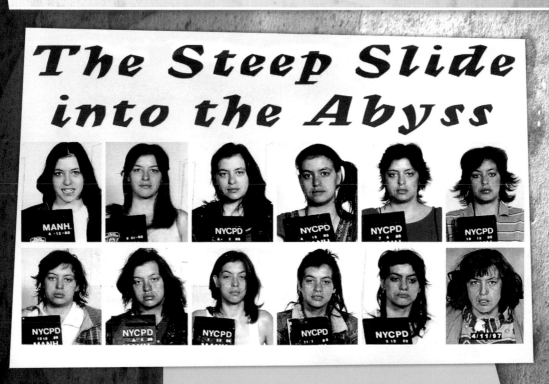

The Steep Slide into the Abyss

Drug use can change the way a person looks. These photos show the change in one addict's appearance.

Other drug effects

The long-term effects of crack, cocaine, LSD, methamphetamines, heroin, and other drugs can be very serious. These drugs can cause permanent damage to the brain, the kidneys, liver, and other organs. A person on drugs may not get the nutrients they need to stay healthy. They may develop wrinkles at a younger age than normal. Drug use can also lead to mental illnesses such as anxiety and paranoia.

It is easy to overdose on recreational drugs.

Drug dangers

Using drugs recreationally is dangerous for many reasons. Because every person's body chemistry is unique, some people may react badly to certain drugs. They may have **seizures,** heart failure, be unable to breathe – and even die. There is no way to predict who will have a bad reaction.

The dosages of recreational drugs are not controlled by a doctor, so it is easy to overdose. Overdoses can result in brain damage or even death. In addition, people who overdose sometimes do not get medical attention because the people around them are also using drugs. Their judgement may be so impaired that they do not realize that their friend is in trouble. They may not want to tell a doctor they have been using an illegal drug.

Case Study

Marissa was just 15 years old when she died from taking Ecstasy at a party. Although she had experimented with other drugs, she had not used Ecstasy before. Soon after taking the pill, Marissa's body went into **convulsions,** and her brain could not get the oxygen it needed. By the time Marissa arrived at the hospital, she was already brain dead.

Most drugs impair judgement and **motor skills.** Some drugs cause people to become depressed or violent. Crimes and accidents are often caused by people using drugs. Drugs that are injected pose an additional risk because people who inject illegal drugs often share needles. Sharing needles with other people can cause the spread of serious diseases such as hepatitis and HIV.

Mixing drugs

Since most recreational drugs are not made legally, they could be mixed with other substances without users knowing. For example, they could be mixed with other drugs or dangerous chemicals. Mixing different recreational drugs can increase their effects, with dangerous consequences. Mixing drugs and alcohol is also dangerous. Many people have died from mixing drugs and alcohol.

A party can become dangerous when drugs are present.

Addicted to drugs

Many drugs change the way the brain works so that the person becomes addicted to the drug. When the person does not get the drug, he or she feels strong **cravings** and will have intense **withdrawal** symptoms. It is very difficult for a person to stop using a drug once he or she has become addicted.

Drug use strains relationships and hurts families.

Top Tips

If you think a friend has a problem with drugs, you may be able to help by talking to him or her. Here are some tips:
- Talking about drugs can be difficult. You may want to talk to a trusted adult first.
- Choose a time when your friend is not using drugs.
- Do not accuse your friend of being an addict. Instead, express your concern about his or her drug use.
- Say what you have seen him or her do when using drugs.
- Be prepared for **denial** and anger.
- Offer to help your friend get the help that he or she needs.

The life of an addict

An addict's whole life becomes focused around getting and using drugs. Since taking drugs is illegal and dangerous, many people lie about their drug use. Drug use among teenagers can make for stressful relationships with parents – and friends. People who are addicted to drugs may become aggressive and lash out at the people around them. They can feel happy one moment and depressed the next.

Heavy drug users may have trouble doing normal daily activities, such as household chores. They may lose their jobs or fail in school. Drugs are expensive, and addicts may steal, beg, or sell drugs themselves to get enough money to buy drugs. People with serious drug problems may fail to eat properly, keep clean, or think of their safety. Some people become so addicted to drugs that they spend most of their time in a drug-induced stupor.

Some teenagers sell drugs to pay for their own drugs.

Recovery from addiction

People who are addicted to drugs are often in denial. Family members or friends may need to help the person to understand that he or she has an addiction problem. Often, people only realize that they have a serious problem when their addiction leads to a crisis, such as being hospitalized or arrested. Young people who think they have a problem with drugs should talk to a parent, teacher, or other trusted adult.

There are many different kinds of treatment programmes. No single treatment will work for everyone. Most people will benefit from a combination of different approaches.

What do you think?

Sometimes drug users who have committed crimes are put into treatment programmes instead of prison. Supporters say that the programmes help people turn their lives around and live productively. Opponents think that the new programmes are soft on crime. Do you think people who abuse drugs should be sent to prison or given treatment?

Sometimes a person needs help to realize that he or she has a problem with drugs.

It may take a crisis such as an overdose to make a person realize they are addicted to drugs.

Detoxification

When drug addicts decide to stop taking drugs, they have to go through **detoxification** to rid their body of the drugs. During detoxification, an addict will experience withdrawal symptoms as his or her body adjusts to living without the drug. Withdrawal symptoms can be severe and may require hospitalization. People in detox may experience depression, anxiety, nausea, vomiting, headache, and even convulsions and hallucinations. In some cases, medications are given to help ease withdrawal systems and return the body to normal functioning.

Cravings can be very strong during this period. Addicts who are not hospitalized may have to be watched constantly to be sure that they are not finding ways to continue to use the drug. This period can take up to several weeks, depending on the drug and how heavily the person is addicted.

Rehabilitation

Programmes for **rehabilitation** are an essential part of the treatment process. Rehabilitation helps recovering drug addicts by addressing emotional issues. It also teaches them new coping skills for staying away from drugs. Most people who do not participate in rehabilitation relapse, or return, back into addiction. Some rehabilitation programmes are designed especially for teenagers and young adults.

People who are heavily addicted to drugs over a long period of time often benefit from inpatient rehabilitation programmes. Recovering addicts live at an inpatient facility for several weeks or months. The controlled environment keeps the person away from drugs and temptation. At the same time, they learn new skills for living without drugs.

Case Study

At the age of 16, Darren tested positive for heroin, cannabis, cocaine, and methamphetamine. He agreed to go to a rehabilitation programme and soon realized that he would not be happy until he stopped using drugs. Darren worked hard to get clean. He made friends with some of the other people in the group and got involved in helping other children stay away from drugs.

Getting support is an important part of recovering from drug addiction.

Outpatient rehabilitation programmes are effective for people who are not heavily addicted and who have strong family and community support. An outpatient facility is a place where recovering addicts go for treatment and support as they learn to live a drug-free life.

Long-term support

A support group or regular visits with a counsellor or therapist help to keep a person from using drugs again. There are support groups especially for teenagers and counsellors who specialize in working with young people.

Unfortunately, even with the best care, some recovered addicts do relapse. When an addict relapses, they must begin treatment again. Although staying away from drugs is difficult, it can be done. Many people who have abused drugs in the past go on to live healthy and happy lives.

Real friends will never pressure you to try drugs.

Saying no to drugs

There are many different kinds of drugs and it can be hard to say no when a friend offers them to you. But remember that using drugs recreationally is illegal and can be very dangerous. Here are some tips for keeping yourself safe:

- Stay away from situations where you know there will be drugs. Do not hang out with people who you know take drugs and stay away from unsupervised parties.

- Find a friend who is also committed to staying off drugs, then stick together. It is much easier to say no if you are not alone.

- Remember: it is okay to just say no; you do not have to give a reason.

- Stand up straight; use a strong voice and clear language.

Here are some different ways to say no, depending on your situation. Try to find a reason that is true for you:

"Not for me, thanks."

"No way, my parents will ground me for life if I get caught doing drugs."

"I know someone who overdosed, so I never take drugs."

It is okay to be rude if someone will not stop pressuring you. Tell them to leave you alone or just walk away. Sometimes it helps to talk to someone you trust, such as your parents or guardians, an older sibling, teacher, or friend. It can be hard to say no, but your real friends will respect your decision not to take drugs.

Drug facts

Drug use among children has increased greatly over the past few years. This includes abusing prescription and over-the-counter drugs as well as taking illegal drugs. Here are some facts you should know:

- Cannabis is the most frequently used illegal drug.

- About 11 percent of 11–15 year olds in the United Kingdom have used cannabis in the last year.

- The maximum sentence for possessing cannabis is two years imprisonment and an unlimited fine.

- The maximum sentence for supplying cannabis (which includes passing a joint to a friend) is 14 years imprisonment and an unlimited fine.

- Solvent abuse accounts for between 70 and 100 deaths in children every year.

- About 4 percent of 11-year-olds reported using solvents in the last year.

- A recent Australian survey of young people ages 16–24 showed that 57 percent of males and 49 percent of females had used cannabis at least once.

- Prescription drugs are not safer than illegal drugs. They can be just as addictive and just as dangerous.

- The most commonly abused prescription drugs are opiates, depressants, and stimulants.

- Random drugs tests are now becoming more common in schools.

- Drugs test can detect cocaine in the urine three days after it was used.

Glossary

addictive describes something that causes the body to become dependent on it

anabolic steroids artificial hormones that cause the muscles and bones to grow

anxiety feeling of worry

cannabis dried leaves or flowers from the hemp plant

coordination ability to move different parts of the body at the same time so that they work together

convulsion sudden, uncontrollable shaking or movement of the body

craving extremely strong desire

denial refusal to accept a truth

depressant substance that slows down the vital systems in the body

detoxification removing a poison from the body

euphoria feeling of intense happiness

flashbacks experiencing the effect of a hallucinogenic drug long after it has worn off

gateway drug drug that is not physically addicting, but may lead to the use of addictive drugs

hallucination something that is seen or heard that is not really there

hallucinogens drugs that cause people to hallucinate

illegal against the law

inhibition feeling of worry or embarrassment that keeps people from doing or saying whatever they want

motor skills ability to use muscles effectively for movement

opiates addictive drugs that come from the opium poppy. Some opiates are used medically to reduce pain.

overdose dangerously large dose of a drug

over-the-counter drug legal medicine that can be bought without a prescription

paranoia intense belief that other people want to harm you

peer pressure social pressure to behave or look a certain way in order to be accepted by a group

prescription drug medicine that can only be legally obtained with instructions from a doctor

rehabilitation return to a healthy condition and way of living

seizure sudden attack of a disease, especially convulsions

solvent product with fumes that can be sniffed in order to get high

stimulants substance that speeds up the vital systems in the body

sudden sniffing death death within minutes of inhaling fumes from a solvent due to heart failure

supplying giving or selling drugs to other people. Includes buying for your friends, passing a joint around friends, and so on.

withdrawal unpleasant physical and emotional symptoms that occur when a person gives up a substance on which he or she was dependent

Further resources

Books

Alex does Drugs, Janine Amos (Cherrytree Books, 2003)

Drugs (What about health), Fiona Waters (Hodder Wayland, 2004)

Drugs (Wise guides), Anita Naik (Hodder Children's Books, 2005)

Websites

Talk to Frank
www.talktofrank.com

Drugscope
www.drugscope.org.uk

Addaction
www.addaction.org.uk

Drugs Info
www.drugs-info.co.uk

Government drugs site
www.drugs.gov.uk

Organizations:

National Treatment Agency
8th Floor, Hercules House
Hercules Road
London SE1 7DU
Tel: 020 7261 8801
E-mail: nta.enquiries@nta-nhs.org.uk

Australian Drug Foundation
Office: 409 King Street, West Melbourne 3003
Postal: PO Box 818, North Melbourne 3051
Tel: 03 9278 8100
E-mail: adf@adf.org.au
Web: www.adf.org.au

Index